Originally published as Pasta—en lidenskap, design by Lise Mosveen
Copyright © Gyldendal Norsk Forlag ASA, Gyldendal Fakta
English edition copyright © 1999 Ten Speed Press
All rights reserved. No part of this book may be reproduced in any form, except
excerpts for the purpose of review, without the written permission of the publish

Ten Speed Press
P.O. Box 7123
Berkeley, California 94707
www.tenspeed.com

Distributed in Canada by Ten Speed Press Canada, in New Zealand by Southern
Publishers Group, in Australia by Simon and Schuster Australia, in South Africa by
Real Books, in Singapore and Malaysia by Berkeley Books, and in the United
Kingdom and Europe by Airlift Books.

A Kirsty Melville book

Library of Congress Cataloging-in-Publication Data
Hensley, Nina Dreyer.
   [Pasta, en lidenskap. English]
   Pasta: a passion / Nina Dreyer Hensley, Jim Hensley, and Paul Løwe.
      p.   cm.
   ISBN 1-58008-106-1 (spiral bound)
   1. Cookery (Pasta) I.Hensley, Jim. II. Løwe, Paul. III. Title.
   TX809.M17H46313 1999
   641.8'22--dc21   99-26363
                                                         CIP

First Printing, 1999
Printed in Norway: PDC Tangen
1 2 3 4 5 6 7 8 9 10 — 03 02 01 00 99

a passion

FEW FOODS ARE AS EASY TO MAKE OR TASTE AS GOOD AS PASTA. A GOOD OLIVE OIL, PASTA, AND A COUPLE OF CANS OF TOMATOES ARE NECESSARIES IN ANY KITCHEN WHERE PEOPLE ARE FOND OF FOOD BUT IN A HURRY. IF YOU EXTEND YOUR COLLECTION WITH FRESH PARMESAN CHEESE, SUN-RIPENED TOMATOES AND BALSAMIC VINEGAR, PREPARING AN OUTSTANDING MEAL WILL BECOME EVEN MORE SIMPLE. PASTA OFFERS YOU COUNTLESS VARIETY THROUGH PLAIN BUT OUTSTANDING RAW MATERIALS THAT MAKE A BIG DIFFERENCE IN FLAVOR. YOU WILL DECIDE THE AMBITION LEVEL, BUT KEEP IN MIND THAT THE BETTER THE RAW MATERIALS, THE BETTER THE OUTCOME WILL TASTE. THIS COOKBOOK IS A TRIBUTE TO PASTA'S MULTITUDE AND SIMPLICITY AND A SOURCE OF INSPIRATION TO HELP YOU EXPLORE NEW, TASTY COMBINATIONS WITH PASTA.

Pasta

NINA DREYER HENSLEY, JIM HENSLEY AND PAUL LØWE

a passion

TEN SPEED PRESS
BERKELEY, CALIFORNIA

CONTENTS

RECIPES

Penne

Ravioli

Tortellini

Fusilli

Tagliatelle

Spaghetti

Linguine

FRESH AND DRIED PASTA

Once, pasta meant only spaghetti and macaroni. Now, you can buy pasta, both fresh and dried, in all kinds of shapes and colors. Most major supermarkets today carry fresh pasta, which is available in various flavors and wonderful colors.

The selection of fresh pasta is often limited to spaghetti, fettuccini, and tagliatelle, but dried pasta is found in all kinds of shapes and sizes. In Italy, dried pasta is generally used with oil-based sauces, while fresh pasta is used with cream- and butter-based sauces. Hollow dried pasta shapes and spaghetti work well with thick, rustic sauces; more delicate pastas are better suited to lighter sauces.

Making pasta yourself can be fun, especially if you don't have access to a source for fresh pasta. We have included a recipe for fresh egg pasta and one for fresh spinach pasta.

Sage

Oregano

Rosemary

HERBS

Fresh or dried herbs are necessary ingredients in pasta sauces. Fresh herbs are usually preferable, but if you only have access to dried ones, you can get good results from these as well. Fresh herbs should be added to the sauce just before serving, whereas dried herbs need to be added earlier in the cooking process. Fresh herbs can be found in most produce markets, and you can grow your own in pots at home.

BASIL

Fresh, ripe tomatoes are basil's best friend, and together they are classically Italian. Basil is one herb that should always be used fresh, as the dried herb has very little flavor. You can freeze fresh basil with a little salt added in order to protect the green color. Basil is used in many pasta sauces and in salads, and is the base for the traditional pesto sauce.

OREGANO

Oregano may be used either fresh or dried, as it keeps its flavor well after drying. Use the dried form in long-cooked sauces. To substitute fresh for dried, or vice versa, use 3 parts fresh to 1 part dried.

Flat-leaf parsley

Thyme

Basil

THYME

Like oregano dried thyme keeps its flavor well. To substitute fresh for dried, or vice versa, use 3 parts fresh to 1 part dried.

FLAT-LEAF PARSLEY

Flat-leaf parsley, sometimes called Italian parsley, has a more intense flavor than curly-leaf parsley. Parsley is used in a myriad of ways, including as a garnish. It should always be used fresh, as it loses most of its flavor when dried.

SAGE

Sage may be used either dried or fresh. Fresh leaves can be sautéed in butter and poured over freshly cooked pasta as a dressing.

ROSEMARY

Rosemary grows wild in the Mediterranean hills and has an intense fragrance. It is particularly suitable for chicken, pork, and lamb.

Asian noodle salad

Serves 6
20 minutes + 30 minutes for marinating

1/2 cup soy sauce

1 tablespoon Thai fish sauce (nam pla)

4 tablespoons Chinese chile sauce

1/4 cup minced fresh cilantro

1 tablespoon grated fresh ginger

Juice of 1 lemon

2 tablespoons teriyaki sauce

12 ounces monkfish or other mild white fish

Olive oil for brushing

1 pound linguine

4 ounces bay shrimp, chopped

1 red bell pepper, seeded, deribbed, and finely chopped

1 yellow bell pepper, seeded, deribbed, and finely chopped

1/2 bunch cilantro, stemmed and coarsely chopped

Stir the soy sauce, fish sauce, chile sauce, minced cilantro, ginger, lemon juice, and teriyaki sauce together in a bowl.

Put the fish in the marinade.

Cover and refrigerate for about 30 minutes.

Remove the fish from the marinade and drain well on paper towels.

Preheat the oven to 350°F.

Brown the fish for 2 minutes on each side in a hot skillet brushed with oil.

Bake the fish with the marinade for about 10 minutes.

Cook the pasta in a large pot of salted boiling water until al dente. Drain.

Gently mix the fish, shrimp, peppers, and chopped cilantro.

Divide the pasta among 6 bowls.

Top with the fish mixture.

Eggplant lasagna

Serves 6

40 minutes

In this unusual "lasagna," linguine, sauce, and eggplant are layered on the plates. Serve with bread and salad.

2 tablespoons plus 1 teaspoon paprika

2 tablespoons minced fresh thyme

1 cup olive oil

3 globe eggplants, cut into 18 1/4-inch-thick slices

1 bunch fresh cilantro, stemmed

1/4 cup plus 3 tablespoons grated Parmesan cheese

1/4 cup pine nuts

5 tablespoons olive oil

5 ounces medium shrimp, peeled and deveined

12 ounces boneless white fish, cut into cubes

1/4 cup dry white wine

1 1/2 cups heavy cream

2 tablespoons minced fresh chives

Salt and freshly ground black pepper to taste

6 ounces linguine, broken roughly into 1-inch pieces

2 tomatoes, peeled and cut into wedges

Mix 2 tablespoons paprika with the thyme and oil.

Brush the eggplant slices with the mixture.

Grill or brown the eggplant slices on each side.

Process the cilantro, 1/4 cup Parmesan, pine nuts, and

cup of olive oil in a food processor until smooth.

Heat the remaining 5 tablespoons oil in a skillet.

Sauté the shrimp and fish until the shrimp

turn pink and the fish is lightly browned.

Transfer the fish and shrimp to a plate.

Stir the wine into the pan.

Cook the wine until reduced by half.

Add the cream and chives.

Add the fish, shrimp, and remaining Parmesan.

Add the salt, pepper, and remaining paprika.

Set aside and keep warm.

Cook the pasta in a large pot of salted boiling water until al dente. Drain.

Gently mix the pasta with the fish mixture.

Put a slice of eggplant on each plate.

Top with some of the fish and pasta mixture.

Repeat to make 3 layers, ending with eggplant.

Garnish with tomato wedges.

Sprinkle a little cilantro pesto around each serving.

Baked pasta

Serves 6 to 8

30 minutes + 60 to 70 minutes for baking

3 tablespoons olive oil

2 cloves garlic, minced

3 (14-ounce) cans tomatoes

Salt, freshly ground black pepper, and sugar to taste

6 tablespoons butter

$^1/_3$ cup flour

$^3/_4$ cup milk

Ground nutmeg to taste

1 package lasagna noodles

1 $^1/_2$ cups freshly grated Parmesan cheese

Heat the oil in a saucepan.

Sauté the garlic until soft.

Add the tomatoes.

Add salt, pepper, and sugar.

Simmer, uncovered, for about 30 minutes, or until thickened.

Set the tomato sauce aside.

Preheat the oven to 350°F.

Melt the butter in a saucepan.

Stir in the flour and cook for 2 minutes.

Stir in the milk.

Bring to a boil, reduce heat, and simmer for about 5 minutes.

Add more milk if the sauce becomes too thick.

Add salt and nutmeg to taste.

Cook the pasta in a large pot of salted boiling water until al dente. Drain.

Place the noodles on a damp towel.

Grease a 10-inch springform pan.

Put a layer of noodles in the bottom of the pan.

Add a layer of white sauce and then a layer of tomato sauce.

Sprinkle with a little Parmesan cheese.

Repeat to make 5 or 6 layers.

Sprinkle with the remaining Parmesan cheese.

Bake the pasta for 50 to 60 minutes, or until golden brown.

Remove from the oven and let sit for 15 minutes.

Cut the pasta into 6-8 servings.

Cannelloni with sausage and tomatoes

Serves 6

50 minutes + time to make fresh pasta

Use either spicy or mild Italian sausage.

¹/₄ **cup olive oil**

8 ounces Italian sausage, casings removed and sausage finely chopped

3 cloves garlic, minced

1 onion, finely chopped

2 (14-ounce) cans chopped tomatoes

Salt and freshly ground black pepper to taste

¹/₂ **cup ricotta cheese or cottage cheese**

¹/₂ **cup freshly grated Parmesan cheese**

1 pound fresh pasta (page 22)

Preheat the oven to 350°F.

Heat half the oil in a skillet.

Add the sausage and sauté for about 5 minutes, or until golden brown.

Heat the remaining oil in a saucepan.

Sauté the garlic and onion until the onion is translucent.

Add the tomatoes, salt, and pepper.

Bring the sauce to a simmer and cook, uncovered, until thickened.

Stir in the ricotta, Parmesan, and sausage.

Set the sauce aside.

Cut the pasta into 18 rectangles, 3 by 4-inch.

Cook the pasta in salted boiling water for 2 minutes. Drain.

Place the pasta on a damp towel.

Spoon the sausage mixture in a ribbon in the center of each pasta rectangle.

Roll each rectangle into a cylinder.

Place the rolls in an oiled pan.

Pour the tomato sauce over them.

Bake in the middle of the oven for about 20 minutes, or until the sauce bubbles.

MOLINO
BORGIOLI
S.R.L.
SEDE E STABILIMENTO
VIA DI PRATO, 24
CALENZANO
(FIRENZE)
SEMOLA
DI GRANO DURO
Peso all'origine netto 50 kg
BORGIOLI S.R.L.
CALENZANO (Firenze)

Fresh pasta

About 2 pounds pasta
20 minutes

4 ¹/₂ cups all-purpose or semolina flour
1 teaspoon salt
5 eggs
6 egg yolks

Put the flour and salt in a large bowl.

Make a well in the center of the flour.

Beat the eggs and egg yolks together and add them to the well.

Stir the eggs into the flour with a fork.

Work the mixture together with your hands.

Scrape the dough out onto a work surface and knead until smooth,
about 8 minutes.

Cut the dough into 12 pieces.

Flatten each piece and fold it into thirds.

For cut pasta, pass each piece through a pasta machine closed 1 notch.

Continue to roll the pasta, narrowing the machine opening 1 notch each time
until all the pasta is rolled thin.

Spread the sheets on towels and let dry for 10 minutes.

Roll each into a flattened roll and cut into strips as desired, 1 inch wide for
pappardelle and ¹/₄ inch wide for tagliatelle.

For filled pasta, pass 1 piece at a time repeatedly through the machine until thin.

Keep all other dough wrapped in plastic.

Do not dry the pasta.

Green cannelloni with mushrooms

Serves 6

50 minutes + time to make fresh pasta

This dish can be prepared up to 24 hours in advance.

8 tablespoons unsalted butter

6 ounces mushrooms

Salt and freshly ground black pepper to taste

$1/3$ cup flour

$1 1/2$ cups milk

$1/2$ cup freshly grated Parmesan cheese

1 egg

1 pound fresh spinach pasta (page 130)

4 ounces diced ham

Preheat the oven to 350°F.

Finely chop the mushrooms.

Melt half the butter in a skillet.

Sauté the mushrooms for about 5 minutes.

Add salt and pepper.

Set aside and let cool.

Melt the remaining 4 tablespoons butter in a saucepan.

Stir in the flour and cook for 2 minutes.

Gradually stir in $3/4$ cup of the milk and simmer until thickened.

Pour half the sauce into another saucepan.

Gradually stir the remaining $3/4$ cup milk into this sauce.

Mix in the Parmesan cheese.

Add salt and pepper.

Combine the mushrooms and the thickest of the white sauces. Let cool.

Stir the egg into the mushroom mixture.

Cut the pasta into 18 rectangles, 3 by 4-inch.

Cook the pasta in salted boiling water. Drain.

Place the pasta on a damp towel.

Spoon a ribbon of the mushroom mixture down

the center of each pasta rectangle.

Roll each rectangle into a cylinder.

Put the rolled pasta in an oiled pan.

Stir a little more milk into the rest of the white sauce if it is very thick.

Pour the sauce over the pasta.

Sprinkle with ham.

Bake in the center of the oven for about 20 minutes,

or until the sauce bubbles and is golden brown.

Hot-and-sour **shrimp pasta**

Serves 6
30 minutes

Sake and Asian sesame oil are available in Asian markets.

1 pound large shrimp, shelled and deveined
3 tablespoons sake
1¹/₂ tablespoons minced fresh ginger
1 teaspoon Asian sesame oil
1 pound tagliatelle
4 tablespoons olive oil
1 red onion, cut into thin slices
2 cloves garlic, minced
1 small red pepper, crushed

Hot-and-Sour Sauce
2 cups chicken broth
¹/₄ cup soy sauce
2 tablespoons sake (rice wine)
2 tablespoons sugar
2 tablespoons Worcestershire sauce
1 teaspoons Asian sesame oil
1 tablespoon cornstarch

Put the shrimp in a bowl with the sake, ginger, and sesame oil.
Let sit for about 15 minutes.
Cook the pasta in a large pot of salted, boiling water until al dente. Drain.
Heat 2 tablespoons of the oil in a saucepan.
Add the shrimp and cook until pink.
Transfer the shrimp to a plate.
Add the remaining 2 tablespoons oil to the pan.
Add the red onion, garlic, and red pepper.
Sauté until the onion is soft. Set aside.
Mix all the sauce ingredients together.
Stir into the vegetables.
Stir constantly until the sauce boils.
Cook the sauce for 2 to 3 minutes, until it thickens.
Gently mix in the shrimp and pasta.
Divide among 6 bowls to serve.

PARMESAN

Parmesan, or Parmigiano, as it is called in Italy, is hard and grainy and has a special nutlike taste. This exquisite cheese is essential in the Italian kitchen. Parmesan comes from the provinces of Parma and Reggio, north of Bologna. Its production is based on time-honored traditions and takes place under strict controls, starting with a mixture of fresh milk with skimmed milk from the evening before. Many countries make Parmesan cheese, but nothing can measure up to Parmigiano-Reggiano from Italy.

Before the cheese is stored, it is marinated in brine for several weeks. Thereafter, it is stored for at least two years. When the cheese has been stored for a year, the "Parmesan police"–an inspector from the *concorzio*–inspects each individual cheese with a hammer and listens for the hollow areas that reveal poor quality. As many as two out of ten cheeses may have to be discarded. Other cheeses normally become somewhat sharper with age, but Parmesan becomes milder. A young Parmesan cheese can be served with fresh fruit, as dessert. Parmesan is used in soups, pastas, and salads. It dries much quicker than other cheeses, so wrap it in parchment paper, then plastic or aluminum foil, before you store it in your refrigerator.

Fresh Parmesan cheese is not inexpensive, but it is worth every penny. The taste is miles away from the grated Parmesan cheese sold in containers.

Lobster ravioli

Serves 6
20 minutes + time to make fresh pasta

Serve this exquisite pasta dish as an appetizer.

1¹/₂ pounds thawed frozen lobster tails

4 ounces salmon fillet, skinned, boned, and cut into bite-sized pieces

2 tablespoon minced fresh flat-leaf parsley

Salt and freshly ground black pepper to taste

8 ounces fresh pasta (page 22)

3 tablespoons unsalted butter

1 head savoy cabbage, cored and shredded

1 cup thinly sliced carrots

1 cup fish stock or clam broth

5 tablespoons olive oil

Remove the lobster from the shells and finely chop the meat.

Put the salmon in a food processor.

Process until the salmon is a smooth purée.

Mix the salmon purée, lobster, and 1 tablespoon parsley in a bowl.

Add salt and pepper.

Roll the mixture into 6 balls.

Cut the pasta into 12 4-inch squares.

Put a lobster ball in the center of 6 squares.

Moisten the edge of the squares. Top each with a second square
and press the edges to seal. To make a circle, trim the edges.

Melt 1¹/₂ tablespoons of the butter in a saucepan.

Sauté the cabbage until limp.

Set aside.

Melt the remaining 1¹/₂ tablespoons butter in the same pan.

Add the carrots and cook until tender.

Set aside.

Boil the stock until reduced by half.

Add the olive oil and remaining parsley.

Cook the ravioli in a large pot of salted gently boiling water until al dente.

Arrange the cabbage on plates.

Put the ravioli on top and place the carrots on top of the ravioli.

Pour some of the reduced stock around each serving.

Pasta baked in paper

Serves 6
40 minutes

³/₄ cup olive oil
1 garlic clove, crushed
1 (14-ounce) can chopped tomatoes, drained
¹/₄ teaspoon red pepper flakes
Salt and freshly ground black pepper to taste
1 pound spaghetti
1 pound fresh tomatoes, peeled and chopped
¹/₂ bunch flat-leaf parsley, stemmed and minced
30 large oil-cured black olives, pitted
Olive oil for sprinkling

Heat the oil in a saucepan.
Sauté the garlic in the oil for 2 minutes.
Remove the garlic, and discard.
Add the canned tomatoes to the pot.
Simmer the tomatoes for about 20 minutes.
Add the pepper flakes, salt, and pepper.
Pour the sauce into a food processor.
Process until the sauce is smooth.
Pour the sauce into a saucepan.
Cook to reduce the sauce by half.
Set aside.
Preheat the oven to 300°F.
Cook the spaghetti in a large pot of salted boiling water until al dente. Drain.
Gently mix the spaghetti, tomato sauce, chopped fresh tomatoes,
most of the parsley, and the olives together.
Cut 6 large sheets of parchment paper.
Divide the pasta among these sheets.
Fold the parchment paper over the top of the pasta and fold the
edges under several times.
Fold the ends of the paper several times to seal tightly.
Bake the packets for 15 minutes.
Carefully loosen the paper so that there is an opening.
Sprinkle a little olive oil and the remaining parsley into the opening.

Pasta with meat ragu

Serves 6

30 minutes + 1 hour for cooking

This pasta, dressed with the celebrated bolognese meat sauce, will keep you warm on cold winter evenings.

4 tablespoons unsalted butter

2 tablespoons finely chopped onion

2 ounces pancetta or bacon, chopped

2 ounces mushrooms, chopped

2 tablespoons minced fresh parsley

2 tablespoons finely chopped carrot

2 tablespoons finely chopped celery

1 bay leaf

12 ounces ground beef

12 ounces ground pork

1 cup dry red wine

1 (14-ounce) can chopped tomatoes

Beef broth (optional)

Salt and freshly ground black pepper to taste

1 pound penne

Melt the butter in a saucepan.

Sauté the onion and pancetta until the onion is translucent.

Add the mushrooms.

Stir in the parsley, carrot, celery, and bay leaf.

Add the beef and pork.

Sauté until the meat is browned.

Add the red wine and tomatoes.

Add salt and pepper.

Cover and cook for about 1 hour, until thickened.

Add a little beef broth if the sauce is too dry.

Cook the penne in a large pot of salted boiling water until al dente. Drain.

Gently mix the sauce and pasta and serve.

Lasagna

Serves 6
60 minutes

This dish is every child's favorite. Lasagna can be made a day in advance and reheated just before serving.

Meat Sauce
2 tablespoons olive oil
8 ounces ground beef
3 ounces bacon, finely chopped
1 onion, finely chopped
2 carrots, finely chopped
1 stalk celery, finely chopped
2 tablespoons minced fresh flat-leaf parsley
2 tablespoons tomato purée
1 1/2 cups chicken broth
Salt and freshly ground black pepper to taste

Béchamel Sauce
2 tablespoons butter
3 tablespoons flour
2 1/2 cups milk
Salt and freshly ground black pepper to taste

1 package lasagna noodles
1 cup freshly grated Parmesan cheese
2 tablespoons butter, cut into bits

Heat the oil in a skillet.
Sauté the ground beef and bacon until browned.
Add the onion, carrots, celery, and parsley.
Sauté until the onion is soft.
Stir in the tomato purée and chicken broth.
Add salt and pepper.
Simmer the sauce for about 20 minutes, or until thickened.
To make the béchamel: Melt the butter in a saucepan.
Stir in the flour and cook for 2 minutes. Gradually stir in the milk.
Cook until thickened. Add salt and pepper to taste.
Preheat the oven to 350°F.
Cook the lasagna noodles in a large pot of salted boiling water until al dente. Drain.
Rinse the noodles under cold water. Drain on a towel.
Layer the noodles, meat sauce, béchamel sauce, and Parmesan in an oiled pan, ending with béchamel and Parmesan. Dot the pieces of butter on the top.
Bake for about 30 minutes, or until golden brown.
Let sit 15 minutes before cutting.

Lasagna stacks

Serves 6
30 minutes

12 ripe tomatoes, peeled and sliced
5 tablespoons olive oil
1 tablespoon balsamic vinegar
$^1/_2$ bunch basil, stemmed and chopped
Salt and freshly ground black pepper to taste
9 lasagna noodles
Olive oil for sprinkling
6 ounces mozzarella, sliced
Pesto for sprinkling (page 155)

Preheat the oven to 375°F.
Put the tomato slices on a plate.
Add the olive oil, balsamic vinegar, basil, salt, and pepper.
Cover the tomatoes with plastic wrap and set aside.
Cook the lasagna noodles in a large pot of salted boiling water for about
8 minutes, or quite al dente. Drain.
Cut the noodles in half crosswise. Add a little oil to the noodles.
Prepare individual lasagna portions in an oiled pan:
Put 1 noodle piece on the bottom, then a couple of tomato slices,
then a slice of mozzarella.
Repeat twice, finishing with a tomato slice. Repeat to make 6 stacks.
Bake the stacks for 8 to 12 minutes, or until the cheese has melted.
Serve sprinkled with pesto.

Linguine with mussels in white wine

Serves 6
30 minutes

Mussels, tomatoes, and pasta are a classic combination. This dish has a light taste, with a little heat added, thanks to the red pepper.

6 pounds mussels, scrubbed and debearded
¹/₃ bottle dry white wine
3 tablespoons olive oil
2 cloves garlic, minced
1 small dried red pepper, crushed
³/₄ cup heavy cream
Salt and freshly ground black pepper to taste
¹/₂ bunch flat-leaf parsley, stemmed and minced
8 ounces linguine

Put the mussels in a pot with the wine and 2 tablespoons of the oil.

Cover and cook over high heat for about 5 minutes, or until the mussels open.

Discard any mussels that do not open.

Let the shells cool to the touch.

Remove three-fourths of the mussels from their shells.

Reserve the cooking broth.

Heat the remaining 1 tablespoon oil in a saucepan and add the garlic and red pepper.

Sauté the garlic until soft.

Add the reserved mussel cooking broth and cream.

Boil the sauce until reduced by half.

Add salt and pepper.

Add the shelled and unshelled mussels and half the parsley.

Cook the linguine in a large pot of salted boiling water until al dente. Drain.

Gently mix the pasta and mussel sauce.

Sprinkle the remaining parsley on top.

Linguine with mussels in red sauce

Serves 6

20 minutes

3 tablespoons olive oil

4 cloves garlic, minced

6 pounds mussels, scrubbed and debearded

1 cup dry white wine

2 tablespoons minced fresh flat-leaf parsley

1 small dried red pepper, seeded and crushed

2 pounds tomatoes, peeled, seeded, and chopped

2 tablespoons minced fresh basil

Salt and freshly ground black pepper to taste

4 ounces linguine

Minced fresh flat-leaf parsley for garnish

Heat 2 tablespoons of the oil in a stockpot.

Sauté 2 cloves garlic until soft.

Add the mussels and wine.

Cover and cook over high heat until the mussels open.

Discard any mussels that do not open.

Let the shells cool to the touch.

Shell the mussels.

Reserve the cooking broth.

Heat the remaining 1 tablespoon oil in a saucepan and

add the remaining garlic and the parsley.

Add the red pepper and tomatoes.

Simmer the sauce for 30 minutes.

Add the mussel cooking broth.

Bring to a boil.

Remove the pan from heat.

Add the mussels and basil.

Add salt and pepper.

Cook the linguine in a large pot of salted boiling water until al dente. Drain.

Gently mix the pasta and sauce in a large bowl.

Sprinkle with a little chopped parsley and serve.

GARLIC

Garlic is an essential ingredient in many Italian dishes. Make certain that your garlic is fresh. The heads should be plump and firm. Store them in a dry place. Stay away from powdered garlic–it's a very poor substitute!

Linguine with gorgonzola and prosciutto

Serves 6
15 minutes

Pick a mild Gorgonzola; look for Gorgonzola dolcelatte. It's a perfect complement to the somewhat salty prosciutto.

1 tablespoon olive oil
2 red onions, in thin slices
4 ounces prosciutto, cut into shreds
4 ounces oil-packed sundried tomatoes, drained and sliced
$^1/_4$ small red pepper, dried and finely chopped
1 $^1/_2$ cups chicken broth
$^1/_2$ cup heavy cream
1 pound linguine
4 ounces Gorgonzola, crumbled
Minced fresh flat-leaf parsley for garnish

Heat the oil in a saucepan.
Sauté the onion until soft.
Add the prosciutto, sundried tomatoes, and red pepper.
Sauté until the prosciutto is crisp.
Add the chicken broth.
Simmer until the broth has almost disappeared.
Stir in the cream.
Cook the linguine in a large pot of salted boiling water until al dente. Drain.
Gently mix the pasta and sauce.
Stir in Gorgonzola and parsley.

Linguine with crab

Serves 6
15 minutes

Use fresh lump or thawed frozen crabmeat for this flavor-filled pasta dish.

12 to 16 ounces crabmeat

1 small jalapeño, seeded and minced

¹/₂ bunch flat-leaf parsley, stemmed and minced

Juice of 2 lemons

2 cloves garlic, minced

1 cup olive oil

1 pound linguine

Salt and freshly ground black pepper to taste

Olive oil for sprinkling

Put the crabmeat in a bowl.

Add the jalapeño, parsley, lemon juice, and garlic.

Mix all the ingredients well.

Pour the olive oil over.

Cook the pasta in a large pot of salted boiling water until al dente.

Drain.

Gently mix the pasta and the crab mixture.

Add salt and pepper.

Serve with olive oil for sprinkling.

Linguine tart with spinach pesto

Serves 4 to 6

10 minutes + 90 minutes for pie shell, 20 minutes for pasta

This is a fun way to serve pasta.

1 ½ cups all-purpose flour

Pinch of salt

⅓ cup butter, cut into pieces

2 to 4 tablespoons cold water

1 ¼ cups olive oil

2 cloves garlic, minced

2 pounds fresh spinach, stemmed

½ cup freshly grated Parmesan cheese

Salt and freshly ground black pepper to taste

1 pound linguine

Freshly grated Parmesan cheese for serving

Mix the flour and salt together.

Cut in the butter with a pastry cutter until coarse crumbs form.

Gradually stir in the water with a fork, to moisten.

Form into a ball with your hands.

Flatten into a disk, wrap in plastic wrap, and refrigerate 1 hour.

Preheat the oven to 350°F.

Roll the dough out to a 12-inch circle.

Fit the dough into a 10-inch pie pan. Trim and flute the edges.

Pierce the bottom with a fork.

Bake for about 30 minutes, or until golden brown.

Heat 6 tablespoons oil in a saucepan.

Sauté the garlic until soft.

Add the spinach and sauté until wilted.

Let the spinach cool.

Squeeze out the water.

Put the spinach, remaining oil, and Parmesan in a food processor.

Process until smooth.

Add salt and pepper.

Cook the linguine in a large pot of salted boiling water until al dente. Drain.

Gently mix the pasta and spinach mixture together.

Add the pasta to the pie shell. Serve with freshly grated Parmesan cheese alongside.

Lobster spaghetti

Serves 6

20 minutes + 30 minutes for marinating

You can use frozen lobster from the supermarket for this dish, although it is always best if you use fresh lobster.

12 to 16 ounces cooked lobster meat

2 cloves garlic

1 teaspoon kosher salt

3/4 cup olive oil

Juice of 3 lemons

1 small dried red pepper, crushed

1 pound spaghetti

1/2 bunch flat-leaf parsley, stemmed and minced

Salt and freshly ground black pepper to taste

Lemon wedges for serving

Cut the lobster meat into bite-sized pieces.

In a large bowl, crush the garlic cloves with the kosher salt.

Add the oil, lemon juice, and red pepper.

Add the lobster meat and marinate for 30 minutes.

Cook the spaghetti in a large pot of salted boiling water until al dente. Drain.

Return the spaghetti to the pot.

Add the lobster meat and marinade.

Heat the mixture through.

Add the parsley, salt, and pepper.

Serve with lemon wedges.

Panzanella

Serves 6
20 minutes

You can use day-old bread for this salad. For a more elegant taste, replace the red wine vinegar with balsamic vinegar.

6 ounces penne
$1/2$ loaf day-old white bread, cut into cubes
2 tablespoons olive oil
2 tomatoes, diced
1 red onion, cut into thin rings
2 tablespoons minced fresh basil
2 tablespoons minced fresh flat-leaf parsley
2 chicken breasts, grilled or sautéed and cut into slices
$1/2$ cup olive oil
3 tablespoons red wine vinegar
Salt and freshly ground black pepper to taste

Preheat the oven to 350°F.
Cook the pasta in a large pot of salted boiling water until al dente. Drain.
Rinse the pasta with cold water.
Mix the bread cubes and oil together.
Put the bread cubes on a baking sheet.
Bake until they are crisp and golden.
Gently mix the pasta, bread, tomatoes, red onion, herbs, and
chicken in a serving bowl.
Whisk the oil and vinegar together.
Pour the dressing over the salad.
Add salt and pepper.
Serve the pasta immediately, so that the bread cubes do not become soft.

Pappardelle with chicken bolognese

Serves 6

30 minutes + 60 minutes for cooking

This classic Tuscan dish has plenty of flavor and a wonderful fragrance.

2 tablespoons olive oil

4 thick slices bacon

4 boneless chicken breasts, cut into small pieces

2 carrots, diced

1 onion, finely chopped

1 stalk celery, finely chopped

2 cloves garlic, minced

2 tablespoons flour

$3/4$ cup dry red wine

$1 1/2$ cups chicken broth

1 tablespoon tomato purée

1 bay leaf

Pinch of sugar

Salt and freshly ground black pepper to taste

1 tablespoon butter

6 ounces mushrooms, sliced

1 pound pappardelle

$1/2$ bunch parsley, stemmed and minced

Heat the oil in a saucepan.

Sauté the bacon and chicken until the bacon is crisp.

Transfer the bacon and the chicken to a bowl and set aside.

Sauté the carrots, onion, celery, and garlic until the onion is golden.

Stir in the flour and cook for 2 minutes.

Add the wine and broth.

Stir in the tomato purée.

Add the bay leaf, sugar, salt, and pepper.

Simmer for about 1 hour, or until thickened.

Melt the butter in a skillet.

Sauté the mushrooms until golden brown.

Cook the pasta in a large pot of salted boiling water until al dente. Drain.

Mix the sauce, pasta, bacon, chicken, and mushrooms together.

Stir in the parsley.

Pappardelle with wild mushrooms

Serves 6
15 minutes

This is an easily made and tasty pasta dish.

1 pound pappardelle
1 tablespoon olive oil
4 ounces pancetta or bacon, minced
1 pound mushrooms, such as chanterelles, porcini, morels,
or shiitakes, chopped
Leaves from 1 head romaine lettuce, coarsely chopped
2 cloves garlic, minced
1 cup chicken broth
Salt and freshly ground black pepper to taste
Freshly grated Parmesan cheese for serving

Cook the pasta in a large pot of salted boiling water until al dente. Drain.
Set the pasta aside and keep warm.
Heat the oil in a skillet.
Sauté the pancetta until crisp.
Remove the pancetta from the pan.
Sauté the mushrooms until soft and golden.
Transfer the mushrooms to a plate.
Add the lettuce and garlic to the pan.
Sauté until the lettuce begins to soften.
Add the mushrooms and broth.
Add salt and pepper.
Stir in the pasta.
Stir in the pancetta.
Serve on a platter sprinkled with the grated Parmesan.

Pasta with mussels, shrimp, and pesto

Serves 6

25 minutes

4 tablespoons olive oil

1 red onion, finely chopped

2 cloves garlic, minced

2 pounds mussels, scrubbed and debearded

¹/₂ cup dry white wine

1 yellow bell pepper, seeded, deribbed, and diced

1 red bell pepper, seeded, deribbed, and diced

8 mushrooms, sliced

5 ounces shrimp, peeled and deveined

1 pound tagliatelle

1 cup pesto (page 155)

Salt and freshly ground black pepper to taste

Fresh basil sprigs, for garnish

Heat 2 tablespoons of the oil in a stockpot.

Sauté the onion and garlic until soft.

Add the mussels.

Add the white wine.

Cover and cook over high heat until the mussels open.

Discard any mussels that do not open.

Let cool to the touch and remove the mussels from the shells, reserving the juice.

Heat the remaining 2 tablespoons oil in a skillet.

Sauté the bell peppers, mushrooms, and shrimp until golden brown.

Cook the pasta in a large pot of salted boiling water until al dente. Drain.

Toss the pasta with the pesto.

Mix the pasta, vegetables, salt, and pepper together.

Mix the mussels into the pasta, together with some of the mussel juice.

Serve pasta on a platter, garnished with basil.

Pasta with ginger and scallops

Serves 6

20 minutes

This aromatic pasta has a strong Asian flavor.

Marinade

6 tablespoons soy sauce

6 tablespoons water

$1/2$ cup sake (rice wine)

4 tablespoons sugar

2 tablespoons minced fresh ginger

$1/2$ teaspoon minced jalapeño (optional)

1 tablespoon cornstarch

6 ounces bay scallops

12 ounces broccoli, cut into florets

1 pound spaghetti or tagliatelle

1 tablespoon olive oil

2 red or green bell peppers, seeded, deribbed, and cut into strips

Combine all the ingredients for the marinade in a small saucepan.

Heat the marinade, stirring constantly, until thickened.

Let cool.

Pour half the marinade into a bowl.

Add the scallops.

Let the scallops marinate at room temperature for 1 hour.

Preheat the broiler.

Cook the broccoli in boiling water for 1 minute.

Rinse the broccoli in cold water.

Thread the scallops onto 12 wooden skewers.

Brush the scallops with the marinade.

Broil the scallops for about 3 minutes on each side, or until lightly browned.

Cook the pasta in a large pot of salted boiling water until al dente. Drain.

Heat the oil in a skillet.

Sauté the bell peppers until tender, about 3 minutes.

Add the marinade and cook for 3 minutes.

Stir in the broccoli and pasta.

Divide the pasta among 6 plates.

Put 2 skewers of scallops on each plate.

Pasta with tomato tapenade

Serves 6
2 hours for tapenade, 10 minutes for pasta

Baking the tomatoes intensifies their taste in this tapenade, which can be prepared one week in advance. It also tastes good on bruschetta and in sauces.

2 pounds plum tomatoes, halves
2 cloves garlic, minced
2 anchovy fillets
2 tablespoons minced fresh flat-leaf parsley
1 tablespoon red wine vinegar
3 tablespoons olive oil
Salt and freshly ground black pepper to taste
1 pound penne, farfalle, or rigatoni
Freshly grated Parmesan cheese

Preheat the oven to 275°F.

Place the tomatoes on a baking sheet lined with aluminum foil.

Sprinkle the garlic over the tomatoes.

Bake the tomatoes for about 1 hour, or until they start to look dry.

Turn them over and continue baking for about 1 hour.

Transfer the tomatoes, garlic, and anchovies to a blender or food processor.

Add the parsley, vinegar, and olive oil and purée.

Add salt and pepper.

Cook the pasta in a large pot of salted boiling water until al dente. Drain.

Gently mix the pasta and tomato tapenade.

Serve with Parmesan cheese alongside.

TOMATOES

Tomatoes have a central place in many of the dishes in this cookbook. A genuine Italian pasta sauce requires perfectly ripe tomatoes. When possible, use meaty plum tomatoes, or an imported brand of canned plum tomatoes. Sundried tomatoes are also used a good deal in Italian food, and are available either dry or packed in oil.

Pasta paella

Serves 6

About 50 minutes

Here is a Spanish version of pasta, using some of the ingredients usually found in paella.

1 tablespoon olive oil

3 cloves garlic, minced

1 onion, finely chopped

4 ounces prosciutto or smoked ham, cut into thin strips

1 red bell pepper, seeded, deribbed, and cut into thin strips

1 plum tomato, chopped

2 tablespoons tomato purée

1 1/2 cups fish stock or clam broth

Salt and freshly ground black pepper to taste

12 ounces orzo or stellini

4 ounces medium shrimp, peeled and deveined

4 ounces squid, cleaned and cut into rings

1/3 cup oil-cured black olives, pitted and sliced

1/2 bunch parsley, stemmed and minced

6 langoustines or lobster tails, cooked

Heat the oil in a saucepan.

Sauté the garlic, onion, and prosciutto until golden.

Add the bell pepper, tomato, tomato purée, and stock.

Cook the sauce until it thickens.

Add salt and pepper.

Cook the pasta in a large pot of salted boiling water until al dente. Drain.

Add the pasta, shrimp, squid, olives, and parsley to the sauce.

Bring the mixture to a simmer.

Serve the pasta in serving bowls with 1 langoustine in each bowl.

Pasta roll

Serves 6

60 minutes

2 tablespoons butter

1 red onion, finely chopped

2 ounces arugula, blanched, squeezed dry, and finely chopped

12 ounces fresh spinach, washed, stemmed, blanched, squeezed dry, and finely chopped

Salt and freshly ground black pepper to taste

2 tablespoons olive oil

3 cloves garlic, minced

8 ounces mushrooms, thinly sliced

12 ounces ricotta or cottage cheese

1 cup freshly grated Parmesan cheese

1 sheet fresh pasta (page 22)

Pesto for serving (page 155)

Melt the butter in the saucepan.

Sauté the onion until soft.

Stir in the arugula, spinach, salt, and pepper.

Set aside.

Heat the oil in a skillet. Sauté the garlic and mushrooms until browned.

Let cool. Finely chop the mushroom mixture.

Put the ricotta in a bowl.

Stir in the spinach mixture, Parmesan, and salt and pepper to taste.

Trim the sheet of pasta to make a rectangle.

Spread the mushroom mixture in a ribbon on 1 long side of the rectangle, leaving a 1-inch margin.

Cover the rest of the rectangle with the spinach mixture, leaving a 1-inch margin.

Roll the pasta to form a large cylinder.

Put the cylinder on a clean muslin cloth and wrap it in the towel as tightly as possible.

Using kitchen twine, tie the towel at the ends of the sausage at intervals, so that it keeps it shape.

Put the sausage in a fish poacher or oblong pot of salted boiling water.

Let the sausage boil gently for about 20 minutes.

Unwrap the sausage.

Cut it into ½-inch-thick slices.

Put 4 to 6 slices of sausage on each plate.

Serve with the Parmesan cheese and pesto.

Pasta salad with shrimp and scallops

Serves 6
20 minutes

Serve this healthy pasta salad with a good white wine such as a Soave Classico from Northern Italy.

12 ounces medium shrimp, peeled and deveined
12 ounces bay scallops
2 cloves garlic, minced
1 teaspoon grated lemon zest
2 tablespoons olive oil
Freshly ground black pepper to taste
12 ounces pasta shells or fusilli
1 red bell pepper, halved lengthwise, seeded, and deribbed
Salt for sprinkling
6 ounces sugar snap peas

Lemon Mayonnaise
¹/₂ cup mayonnaise
¹/₂ cup sour cream
1¹/₂ teaspoons freshly squeezed lemon juice
1 tablespoon minced fresh flat-leaf parsley

Leaves from 1 large head romaine lettuce, cut into thick shreds
Lime or lemon wedges for garnish

Mix the shrimp, scallops, garlic, zest, oil, and ground pepper in a bowl.
Cover and refrigerate for 2 to 4 hours.
Preheat the broiler.
Cook the pasta in a large pot of salted boiling water. Drain.
Rinse the pasta in cold water. Drain.
Broil the bell pepper until the skin is evenly blackened.
Put the pepper in a plastic bag and let sit for 10 minutes.
Remove the skin and finely chop the pepper.
Sprinkle a little salt on the shrimp and scallops.
Broil the shrimp and scallops for about 2 minutes on each side, or until the shrimp are pink and the scallops are opaque.
Cook the snap peas in salted boiling water for 2 minutes. Drain.
To make the mayonnaise, mix all of the ingredients in a large bowl.
Stir in the pasta, peppers, peas, shrimp, and scallops.
Make a bed of romaine in a salad bowl or on a platter.
Top with the salad.
Garnish with wedges of lime or lemon.

Pasta salad with tomatoes and balsamic syrup

Serves 6
20 minutes

8 ounces large rigato or penne
4 tablespoons olive oil

Balsamic Syrup
3 tablespoons olive oil
3 scallions, finely chopped
³/₄ cup dry red wine
³/₄ cup chicken broth
¹/₂ cup balsamic vinegar
1 tablespoon brown sugar (optional)

6 large, ripe plum tomatoes, peeled and chopped
¹/₂ bunch basil, stemmed and finely chopped
Salt and freshly ground black pepper to taste
Extra virgin olive oil for sprinkling

Cook the pasta in a large pot of salted boiling water until al dente. Drain.
Sprinkle the olive oil over the pasta and set aside.
To make the syrup: Heat the oil in a saucepan.
Sauté the scallions until soft.
Add the red wine and broth.
Cook to reduce the wine by half.
Add the balsamic vinegar.
Cook to reduce the liquid by half.
Taste and add brown sugar, if desired.
Set the sauce aside and let cool.
Mix the pasta and tomatoes.
Place the pasta on plates or in a large bowl.
Stir in the basil.
Add salt and pepper.
Pour the balsamic syrup over the pasta.
Sprinkle with a little bit of olive oil.

Pasta salad with mozzarella and tomatoes

Serves 6

15 minutes + 15 minutes to sit

*Tomatoes and mozzarella were made to go together. Use the best ripe
tomatoes you can find. Serve this with rustic Italian bread.*

2 bunches basil, stemmed

1/2 bunch flat-leaf parsley, stemmed

3 tablespoons minced fresh chives

2 cloves garlic, minced

6 tablespoons olive oil

3 tomatoes, peeled and diced

Salt and freshly ground black pepper to taste

1 pound penne

1 cup diced mozzarella

Balsamic vinegar for sprinkling

Blanch the basil in a pot of boiling water for 10 seconds.

Rinse the basil under cold water.

Squeeze out all the water.

Combine the basil, parsley, chives, garlic, and olive oil in a food processor.

Purée until smooth.

Mix the tomatoes with the basil mixture.

Add salt and pepper.

Cook the pasta in a large pot of salted boiling water until al dente. Drain.

Rinse the pasta under cold water. Drain well.

Mix the pasta, mozzarella, and tomato mixture in a large bowl.

Sprinkle with a few drops of balsamic vinegar.

Let sit for 15 minutes before serving.

Pasta salad with pesto

Serves 6
20 minutes

A highlight of summer, this salad is easy to make and delicious to eat.

4 ounces sugar snap peas, halved crosswise
1 chicken, grilled
¹/₄ cup oil-packed sundried tomatoes, drained and chopped
1 large red onion, finely chopped
¹/₂ bunch flat-leaf parsley, stemmed and chopped
¹/₄ cup black olives, pitted
1 pound penne
¹/₂ cup olive oil
1 cup pesto (page 155)
Salt and freshly ground black pepper to taste

Cook the peas in salted boiling water for 2 minutes. Drain.
Bone and skin the chicken.
Cut the meat into pieces.
Mix the chicken, peas, sundried tomatoes, red onion, parsley, and olives in a large bowl.
Cook the pasta in a large pot of salted boiling water until al dente. Drain.
Rinse the pasta with cold water. Drain well.
Gently mix the pasta with the other ingredients in a bowl.
Stir in the olive oil and pesto.
Add salt and pepper.

Pasta with vegetables

Serves 6

30 minutes + 1 hour for marinade

This crisp and colorful salad is good for a summer lunch.

1 pound green beans

8 ounces shelling beans, shelled

1 small yellow crookneck squash, cut into thin sticks

1 carrot, thinly sliced

¹/₂ red jalapeño, seeded and minced

1 yellow bell pepper, seeded, deribbed, and chopped

1 tablespoon sugar

¹/₄ teaspoon fennel seeds

Pinch of salt

¹/₂ cup white wine vinegar

2 tablespoons water

¹/₂ cup olive oil

1 pound orecchiette or pasta shells

Salt and freshly ground black pepper to taste

Cook the green beans and shelling beans in salted boiling water for 3 minutes.

Rinse the beans in cold water.

Blanch the squash, carrot, jalapeño, and bell pepper in salted boiling water for 30 seconds. Drain.

Rinse the vegetables in cold water. Drain.

Combine all the vegetables in a bowl.

Combine the sugar, fennel, salt, vinegar, and water in a saucepan.

Bring to a boil and stir until the sugar dissolves.

Pour the sauce and olive oil over the vegetables.

Let the vegetables sit in the sauce for about 1 hour.

Cook the pasta in a large pot of salted boiling water until al dente. Drain.

Mix the pasta and vegetables.

Add salt and pepper.

Penne alla carbonara

Serves 6
15 minutes

Carbonara is a classic pasta dish flavored with pancetta and Parmesan cheese.

1 tablespoon olive oil

6 ounces pancetta or bacon, finely chopped

6 egg yolks

$^1/_2$ cup heavy cream

1 $^1/_2$ cups freshly grated Parmesan cheese

Salt and freshly ground black pepper to taste

8 ounces penne

2 tablespoons minced fresh flat-leaf parsley

Heat the oil in a skillet.

Sauté the pancetta until crisp.

Beat the egg yolks and cream together.

Add half of the Parmesan cheese.

Add salt and pepper.

Cook the pasta in a large pot of salted boiling water until al dente. Drain.

Mix the pasta and pancetta.

Stir in the sauce.

Add the remaining Parmesan cheese, parsley, and pepper.

Toss gently.

Penne with balsamic vinegar

Serves 6

15 minutes + 40 minutes for cooking

Use a good, aged balsamic vinegar–ten years or older–for this dish.

2 tablespoons plus ³/₄ cup olive oil

2 cloves garlic, minced

1 ³/₄ pounds tomatoes, peeled and chopped

¹/₂ bunch basil, stemmed and chopped

Salt and freshly ground black pepper to taste

8 ounces penne

4 tablespoons balsamic vinegar

1 teaspoon packed brown sugar

1 cup freshly grated Parmesan cheese

Heat the 2 tablespoons oil in a saucepan.

Sauté the garlic until soft.

Add one quarter of the tomatoes and one quarter of the basil.

Cook, stirring frequently, for 30 to 40 minutes, or until thickened.

Add salt and pepper.

Add the remaining tomatoes and basil.

Cook the pasta in a large pot of salted boiling water until al dente. Drain.

Return the pasta to the pot. Add ³/₄ cup olive oil.

Heat the mixture and stir in the balsamic vinegar and brown sugar.

Cook, stirring constantly, until well mixed.

Sprinkle half the Parmesan cheese over the mixture and stir in the tomato sauce.

Pass remaining cheese when serving.

Penne with prosciutto

Serves 6
20 minutes

Try to find imported prosciutto for this dish.

2 tablespoons olive oil

6 ounces prosciutto, cut into shreds, or smoked ham, finely diced

1 large red onion, finely chopped

2 tablespoons minced fresh thyme

$^1/_2$ cup dry red wine

2 (14-ounce) cans chopped tomatoes

Salt and freshly ground black pepper to taste

12 ounces penne

Freshly grated Parmesan cheese for serving

Heat the oil in a saucepan.

Sauté the prosciutto until crisp.

Add the onion and thyme.

Sauté the onion until golden.

Add the red wine, tomatoes, salt, and pepper.

Simmer the sauce, stirring occasionally, for 45 minutes.

Cook the pasta in a large pot of salted boiling water until al dente. Drain.

Put the pasta in a large bowl and add the sauce.

Stir the sauce gently into the pasta.

Serve with Parmesan cheese alongside.

Penne with broccoli and green olives

Serves 6
20 minutes

A robustly flavored pasta, this dish combines a variety of interesting tastes.

2 pounds broccoli, cut into florets
2 tablespoons olive oil
2 red onions, cut into thin slices
2 cloves garlic, minced
10 anchovy fillets, chopped
1 cup (5 ounces) pine nuts
1 cup green olives, pitted
Salt and freshly ground black pepper to taste
1 pound penne
¹/₂ bunch basil, stemmed and chopped
Freshly grated Parmesan cheese for serving
Extra virgin olive oil for serving

Cook the broccoli in salted boiling water to cover for 2 to 3 minutes.
Drain, reserving the water.
Heat the oil in a saucepan.
Sauté the onions until soft.
Add the garlic and anchovies.
Sauté until the anchovies have melted.
Add 4 tablespoons of the reserved broccoli water.
Add the broccoli.
Cook for about 5 minutes.
Add the pine nuts and olives.
Turn the heat to low and cook for 5 minutes.
Add salt and pepper.
Cook the penne in a large pot of salted boiling water until al dente. Drain.
Gently mix the sauce, penne, and basil in a bowl.
Serve with Parmesan cheese and olive oil for sprinkling.

Penne with olive and caper tapenade

Serves 6
20 minutes

Olive and caper tapenade is a pungent and richly flavored sauce for penne.
Serve this dish with a healthy Italian white wine, such as Oriveto Classico.

3 tablespoons chopped fresh mint
3 tablespoons capers, drained
2 cloves garlic, minced
$1/2$ teaspoon grated lemon zest
Pinch of red pepper flakes
4 tablespoons olive oil
$1/3$ cup green olives, pitted
Salt and freshly ground black pepper to taste
1 pound penne or tagliatelle
1 cup freshly grated Parmesan cheese

Combine the mint, capers, garlic, lemon zest, pepper flakes, and
olive oil in a food processor.
Process until smooth.
Add the olives.
Process to a coarse paste.
Add salt and pepper.
Cook the pasta in a large pot of salted boiling water until al dente. Drain.
Gently mix the pasta and pesto together in a large bowl.
Stir in the Parmesan and serve.

Pappardelle with artichokes, sundried tomatoes, and garlic oil

Serves 6

20 minutes

Italy's national colors were the inspiration for this dish: The red tomatoes, green artichokes, and white pasta combine colors and tastes from the land of the sun.

4 tablespoons plus $3/4$ cup olive oil

6 cloves garlic, minced

$1/2$ teaspoon salt

1 teaspoon red pepper flakes

1 (10-ounce) package frozen artichoke hearts

1 pound pappardelle

1 tablespoon olive oil

$1/2$ cup oil-packed sundried tomatoes, drained and chopped

$1/2$ cup freshly grated Parmesan cheese

2 tablespoons pine nuts

Minced fresh basil for sprinkling

Heat the 4 tablespoons olive oil in a saucepan.

Sauté the garlic, salt, and pepper flakes until the garlic is soft.

Let cool.

Pour in the $3/4$ cup oil.

Cook the artichoke hearts in salted boiling water to cover for 3 minutes. Drain.

Cut the artichoke hearts in half.

Cook the pasta in a large pot of salted boiling water until al dente. Drain.

Heat the one tablespoon of oil in a skillet.

Sauté the artichoke hearts until lightly browned.

Stir in the sundried tomatoes.

Stir the tomato sauce and pasta together.

Pour the garlic mixture over.

Sprinkle the Parmesan, pine nuts, and basil over the pasta.

Toss gently.

Penne with squash and ricotta

Serves 6
15 minutes

Try to find baby zucchini for this dish.

2 pounds mixed green and yellow baby zucchini
2 tablespoons olive oil
4 cloves garlic, minced
1 pound penne
½ bunch basil, stemmed and minced
1½ cups (12 ounces) ricotta cheese
Salt and freshly ground black pepper to taste
Freshly ground Parmesan for serving

Cook the zucchini in a large pot of salted boiling water for 2 minutes.
Drain.
Let cool.
Cut the zucchini into ½-inch-thick slices.
Heat the oil in a skillet.
Sauté the garlic until soft, but not brown.
Add the zucchini slices and sauté until lightly browned.
Cook the penne in a large pot of salted boiling water until al dente. Drain.
Mix the penne, zucchini, and basil together.
Stir in the ricotta.
Add salt and pepper.
Serve with Parmesan cheese alongside.

OLIVE OIL

Olive oil is the basis for most Mediterranean cuisines. The quality of olive oil is determined by the harvesting method and the pressing. Flavor nuances and color vary, depending on climate, soil, and the olives.

The best olive oil is extra virgin oil, which is made by cold-pressing fully ripened olives and has an acid content of less than 1 percent. It is rich in flavor and adds an outstanding flavor to food.

Penne
with sausage

Serves 6

40 minutes

This is a tasty and filling dish. Use either mild or spicy Italian sausage.

2 tablespoons olive oil

2 small red onions, finely chopped

5 Italian sausages, casings removed and sausage finely chopped

2 tablespoons minced fresh rosemary

2 bay leaves

1 small dried red pepper, crushed

2 (14-ounce) cans chopped tomatoes

Salt and freshly ground black pepper to taste

8 ounces penne

³/₄ cup heavy cream

1 cup freshly grated Parmesan cheese

Heat the oil in a large skillet.

Sauté the onions until soft.

Add the sausage, rosemary, bay leaves, and red pepper.

Mix the ingredients well.

Sauté the sausage until lightly browned.

Pour off all the fat from the pan.

Add the tomatoes, stir well, and bring to a boil.

Remove the pan from the heat.

Cook the pasta in a large pot of salted boiling water until al dente. Drain.

Add the cream to the sausage mixture.

Gently mix the sauce, pasta, and half the Parmesan cheese together.

Serve with the remainder of the Parmesan cheese alongside.

Penne with tuna

Serves 6
30 minutes

Use fresh tuna for this pasta-the flavor is totally different from that of canned.

4 to 5 stalks fresh mint sprigs, finely chopped
2 teaspoons grated lemon zest
1 tablespoon olive oil
1 pound fresh tuna fillets
2 tablespoons olive oil
1 yellow bell pepper, seeded, deribbed, and cut into strips
1 red bell pepper, seeded, deribbed, and cut into strips
1 red onion, cut into thin slices
Salt and freshly ground black pepper to taste
1 pound penne
2 tablespoons balsamic vinegar
1 tablespoon unsalted butter
Dash of soy sauce

Mix the mint, lemon zest, and olive oil in a bowl.
Brush the mixture onto the tuna.
Set the tuna aside in a cool place.
Heat the oil in a skillet.
Sauté the bell peppers for about 3 minutes.
Add the onion, salt, and pepper.
Sauté until the peppers are lightly browned.
Preheat the broiler.
Cook the pasta in a large pot of salted boiling water until al dente. Drain.
Set the pasta aside and keep warm.
Scrape the marinade from the tuna and reserve the marinade.
Broil the tuna for 2 minutes on each side until medium rare.
Let the tuna sit on a cutting board for 5 minutes.
Cut the fish into 1/2-inch-thick slices.
Combine the vegetables, reserved marinade, balsamic vinegar,
and butter in a saucepan.
Bring to a boil, reduce heat, and simmer for 3 minutes.
Gently stir the mixture into the pasta.
Divide the pasta among 6 plates.
Put a few slices of tuna on each plate.
Sprinkle a few drops of soy sauce on top before serving.

SALT

There are few worse things in the world than pasta that has been cooked too long! Perfectly cooked pasta is al dente, which means "to the tooth," or cooked through but still firm and slightly chewy.

Always cook pasta in plenty of water in a large pot, so the pasta will have room to expand. When the water comes to a full boil, add 2 tablespoons of sea salt or kosher salt. Then add the pasta.

Pasta should go into the pot right before being served. Fresh pasta is usually done 2 or 3 minutes after the water returns to a boil. Filled pasta, such as ravioli, is usually done about 2 minutes after it has floated to the surface. Dried pasta usually takes 10 minutes to cook. Always test a piece of pasta to make sure it is properly cooked. Gently stir pasta with a wooden spoon after adding it to the pot and once or twice while cooking so that the pasta does not get stuck on the bottom of the pot.

When cooking spaghetti, hold on to the top of the pasta while the bottom gradually sinks into the pot, rather than breaking the strands in two. Serve freshly cooked; if it is allowed to sit and cool, it will become a glued-together mass. Don't rinse cooked pasta unless you are planning to use it cold in a pasta salad.

Spaghetti with tomatoes and arugula

Serves 6

15 minutes

2 tablespoons olive oil

¹/₄ teaspoon red pepper flakes

2 cloves garlic, minced

6 tomatoes

1 pound spaghetti

5 tablespoons minced fresh basil

Salt and freshly ground black pepper to taste

1 bunch arugula, coarsely chopped

Heat the oil in a saucepan.

Sauté the pepper flakes and garlic for 2 minutes.

Remove the stems of the tomatoes and cut an X on the bottom of each tomato.

Blanch the tomatoes in a large pot of boiling water for 1 minute.

Peel the tomatoes and cut them in half crosswise.

Squeeze and shake out the seeds. Coarsely chop the tomatoes.

Add half of the tomatoes to the garlic mixture.

Simmer the sauce for about 10 minutes, stirring frequently.

Cook the spaghetti in a large pot of salted boiling water until al dente. Drain.

Gently mix the sauce, spaghetti, and basil together.

Add salt and pepper.

Divide the spaghetti among 6 plates.

Make a pile of arugula in the center of each serving.

Sprinkle with the remaining chopped tomatoes.

Ravioli with browned sage

Serves 6
15 minutes

This is a tasty and simple way to prepare ravioli. The leftover sage oil can be used as a dressing for salads.

About 30 fresh sage leaves
1 cup olive oil
1 pound fresh cheese-, mushroom-, or spinach-filled ravioli
Freshly ground black pepper to taste

Make sure the sage leaves are totally dry.
Heat the oil in a small, deep pot.
Dip a wooden spoon into the oil. When bubbles form around it,
the oil is hot enough to brown the sage leaves.
Add the sage and cook about 10 seconds, or until lightly browned.
Using a slotted spoon, transfer the leaves to paper towels to drain.
Set the oil aside.
Cook the ravioli in a large pot of salted boiling water until al dente. Drain.
Return the ravioli to the pot.
Crush half of the sage leaves and gently mix with the ravioli.
Mix in a little bit of the oil.
Add pepper.
Divide the pasta among 6 plates.
Garnish with the remaining sage leaves.

Ravioli filled with smoked salmon

Serves 6

25 minutes + time to make fresh pasta

8 ounces smoked salmon, finely chopped

1/2 cup ricotta cheese or cottage cheese

Salt and freshly ground black pepper to taste

3 egg yolks, beaten

1 1/2 cups cream

2 tablespoons minced fresh flat-leaf parsley

1 pound fresh pasta (page 22)

Olive oil and fennel seeds for sprinkling

Stir the smoked salmon and ricotta cheese
together in a bowl.
Add salt and pepper.
Stir in the egg yolks, cream, and parsley.
Cut the pasta into strips 2 inches wide.
Put 1 teaspoon filling on each strip,
at 2-inch intervals.

Moisten the
edges and
the spaces
between the
mounds of
filling.

Top with a second
strip of pasta.
Use a ravioli cutter to seal
and cut the ravioli.

Put the ravioli on a towel that has
been lightly sprinkled with flour.
Cook the ravioli in a large pot of
salted boiling water until al dente.
Drain.
Sprinkle a little olive oil and
some fennel seeds over
each before serving.

Tagliatelle with shrimp and calamari

Serves 6
20 minutes + 1 hour for marinating

18 jumbo shrimp, peeled and deveined
12 ounces squid, cleaned and cut into rings
4 tablespoons olive oil
Juice of 1 lemon
Salt and freshly ground black pepper to taste
1 pound tagliatelle
1/3 cup unsalted butter
1/2 bunch flat-leaf parsley, stemmed and minced
Olive oil for sprinkling

Combine the shrimp and calamari in a bowl.

Stir in the olive oil, lemon juice, salt, and pepper.

Let the seafood sit in a cool place for about 30 minutes.

Thread the shrimp and calamari onto skewers.

Heat the oil in a skillet.

Sauté the shrimp skewers for about 2 minutes.

Meanwhile, cook the tagliatelle in a large pot of salted boiling water until al dente. Drain.

Mix the tagliatelle, butter, and parsley together well.

Divide the pasta among 6 plates.

Put 1 skewer on each plate.

Serve the pasta with extra olive oil for sprinkling.

Sesame noodles

Serves 6
20 minutes

This recipe makes extra dressing, which can be kept in the refrigerator for about two weeks.

Sesame Dressing
8 cloves garlic, halved lengthwise
1 tablespoon minced fresh ginger
7 tablespoons tahini (sesame paste)
1 1/2 tablespoons sesame oil
5 tablespoons soy sauce
1/2 cup sake (rice wine)
1 tablespoon Worcestershire sauce
1 1/2 tablespoons sugar
6 tablespoons chicken broth

1 pound linguine
2 cucumbers, cut into thin slices with a cheese slicer or mandoline
1 red bell pepper, seeded, deribbed, and cut into thin slices
1 ounce bean sprouts
1 chicken, grilled, skinned, boned, and cut into slices
1 scallion, thinly sliced
2 tablespoons sesame seeds

To make the dressing: Combine all the dressing ingredients in a food processor.
Process until thick and creamy.
If the consistency is too thin, add more tahini.
Cook the linguine in a large pot of salted boiling water until al dente. Drain.
Gently stir the pasta, cucumbers, bell pepper, and bean sprouts together.
Serve on a platter or divide among 6 plates.
Make a well in the center and add the chicken.
Sprinkle the scallion and sesame seeds over.
Serve with the sesame dressing alongside.

Spaghetti with clams in white wine sauce

Serves 6
20 minutes

Mussels may be substituted for the clams.

$^1/_2$ **cup olive oil**

1 cup dry white wine

2 cloves garlic, sliced

1 small dried red pepper, crushed

2 pounds clams, scrubbed

2 shallots, minced

8 ounces spaghetti or linguine

2 tablespoons minced fresh flat-leaf parsley

Salt and freshly ground black pepper to taste

Pour one third of the oil into a stockpot.

Add the wine, 1 clove garlic, and the red pepper.

Add the clams, cover, and cook over high heat until the clams open.

Discard any clams that do not open.

Shell the clams, putting the meat and juice in a large bowl.

Heat the remaining oil in a saucepan.

Sauté the shallots and the remaining garlic until soft.

Add the clam meat, juice, and broth from the stockpot.

Set aside and keep warm.

Cook the spaghetti in a large pot of salted boiling water until al dente. Drain.

Put the spaghetti in a bowl and gently stir in the clam mixture.

Stir in the parsley, salt, and pepper.

Spaghetti with calamari

Serves 6

15 minutes

Take care not to overcook the squid, or it will become tough.

1 pound spaghetti

5 tablespoons olive oil

3 cloves garlic, minced

1 red jalapeño, seeded and minced

8 to 10 small squid, cleaned and cut into $1/4$-inch-thick rings

1 cup dry white wine

$1/2$ bunch flat-leaf parsley, stemmed and minced

Salt and freshly ground black pepper to taste

Cook the spaghetti in a large pot of salted boiling water until al dente. Drain.

Meanwhile, heat the oil in a saucepan.

Sauté the garlic for 2 minutes.

Add the jalapeño and squid.

Sauté for about 30 seconds.

Add the white wine and half of the parsley.

Add salt and pepper.

Gently mix the sauce and spaghetti together in a bowl.

Garnish with the remaining parsley.

Spaghetti with shrimp and garlic

Serves 6
15 minutes

This flavorful pasta is easy to make. You can vary the heat of the dish by adding more or less chile.

1/2 cup olive oil
3 cloves garlic, minced
12 ounces medium shrimp, peeled and deveined
1/2 red jalapeño, minced
1/2 bunch flat-leaf parsley, stemmed and minced
12 cherry tomatoes, halved
1 pound spaghetti
Olive oil for sprinkling

Heat the oil in a saucepan.
Sauté the garlic until soft.
Add the shrimp and chile.
Sauté for 2 or 3 minutes, or until the shrimp are pink.
Stir in the parsley and tomatoes.
Cook the spaghetti in a large pot of salted boiling water until al dente. Drain.
Gently mix the spaghetti and the shrimp mixture together.
Serve the pasta with olive oil for sprinkling.

Spaghetti with oregano and cherry tomatoes

Serves 6
15 minutes

A mixture of fresh and dry oregano makes this spaghetti dish exciting.

7 to 8 fresh oregano sprigs, minced
2 tablespoons dried oregano, crushed in a mortar
20 cherry tomatoes, halved
1 cup extra virgin olive oil
Salt and freshly ground black pepper to taste
12 ounces spaghetti

Mix the fresh and dried oregano together.
Combine the tomatoes, oil, salt, and pepper.
Cook the spaghetti in a large pot of salted boiling water until al dente. Drain.
Drain the tomatoes, reserving the oil. Add the reserved oil to the spaghetti.
Add the oregano mixture and mix well.
Return the spaghetti to the pot.
Divide the pasta among 6 plates.
Put the marinated tomatoes on top of the pasta.

Spaghetti with arugula and ricotta cheese

Serves 6

15 minutes

*For a different, but still very good taste, substitute spinach leaves
for the arugula.*

2 pounds arugula or spinach leaves

2 tablespoons plus 1/2 cup olive oil

3 cloves garlic, coarsely chopped

4 tablespoons coarsely chopped fresh basil

1 red jalapeño, seeded and minced

Salt and freshly ground black pepper to taste

12 ounces spaghetti

1 cup ricotta cheese or cottage cheese

Coarsely chop half of the arugula.

Heat the 2 tablespoons oil in a saucepan.

Sauté the garlic until soft.

Add the basil and the whole arugula leaves.

Cover and cook for 2 to 3 minutes.

Transfer the mixture to a food processor.

Process to a coarse paste.

Add half of the chopped arugula, the jalapeño, salt, pepper,
and the 1/2 cup olive oil.

Process to a smooth sauce.

Cook the spaghetti in a large pot of salted boiling water until al dente. Drain.

Gently mix the spaghetti and sauce together.

Stir the ricotta with a fork.

Stir the ricotta and the remaining chopped arugula gently into the spaghetti.

BALSAMIC VINEGAR

Balsamic vinegar, which originated in Modena and Emilia, north of Bologna, is made from the juice of pressed grapes. The liquid is reduced in copper cauldrons, then poured into wooden barrels to age. Inexpensive balsamic is aged for about two years, while more expensive vinegars are aged from twelve to fifteen years. Some very expensive balsamics are aged for as long as fifty years. The older the balsamic vinegar is, the darker the color. It will also be somewhat sweeter and richer in flavor. Sometimes only a couple of drops of fine aged balsamic is enough to render the characteristic taste. Balsamic vinegar may be sprinkled over food and used in sauces, dressings, and soups. It is even good on fresh fruit; try sprinkling it on strawberries.

Spaghetti with lemon and basil

Serves 6
15 minutes

This is a fresh, delicious dish. Try to find unsprayed lemons so that
a small piece of zest can be grated into the sauce just before serving.

12 ounces spaghetti
Juice of 2 lemons
$3/4$ cup olive oil
1 cup freshly grated Parmesan cheese
Salt and freshly ground black pepper to taste
$1/2$ bunch basil, stemmed and minced
2 tablespoons parsley, chopped
1 tablespoon grated lemon zest

Cook the spaghetti in a large pot of salted boiling water until al dente. Drain.
Return the spaghetti to the pot.
Whisk the lemon juice and olive oil together.
Stir in the Parmesan cheese until the sauce is thick and creamy.
Add salt and pepper.
Gently mix the spaghetti and sauce together.
Gently stir in the basil, parsley, and lemon zest.

Fresh spinach pasta

Makes 2 pounds fresh pasta
20 minutes

4 ¹/₂ cups all-purpose or semolina flour
2 eggs
8 egg yolks
1 cup cooked spinach, squeezed dry and minced
1 teaspoon salt

Pour the flour into a bowl.
Make a well in the center.
Beat the eggs, egg yolks, spinach, and salt together.
Pour into the well.
Stir the mixture into the flour with a fork.
Work the mixture together with your hands.
Scrape the dough out onto a work surface
and knead until smooth, about 8 minutes.
Cut the dough into 12 pieces.
Flatten each piece and
fold it into thirds.
For cut pasta,
pass each piece
through a pasta
machine closed
1 notch.
Continue to roll the
pasta, narrowing
the machine opening
1 notch each time
until all the pasta is
rolled thin.

Spread the sheets on towels and let dry for 10 minutes.

Roll each into a flattened roll and cut into strips as desired, 1 inch wide for pappardelle and 1/4 inch wide for tagliatelle.

For filled pasta, pass 1 piece at a time repeatedly through the machine until thin.

Keep all other dough wrapped in plastic.

Do not dry the pasta.

Fried pasta

Serves 6
20 minutes

5 tablespoons plus 5 teaspoons olive oil

4 cloves garlic, thinly sliced

12 anchovy fillets, halved

3 tablespoons minced fresh flat-leaf parsley

1 pound linguine or spaghetti

Freshly ground black pepper to taste

Marinated peppers (page 158)

Heat the 5 tablespoons oil in a small saucepan.

Sauté the garlic until soft.

Transfer the garlic to a bowl.

Sauté the anchovy fillets in the oil for 1 minute.

Mix the anchovies, oil, garlic, and parsley together.

Cook the pasta in a large pot of salted boiling water until al dente. Drain.

Mix the pasta with the garlic mixture.

Add pepper.

Heat the 5 teaspoons oil in a skillet.

Divide the pasta into 6 equal portions.

Add 1 portion to the pan and press the pasta flat with a fork.

Cook until browned and crisp on the bottom.

Turn the pasta carefully, using a spatula.

Cook the pasta on the other side until browned and crisp.

Serve with the marinated peppers.

Tagliatelle with asparagus and herbs

Serves 6
15 minutes

1¼ **pounds fresh thin asparagus, trimmed**

1½ **cups heavy cream**

4 **cloves garlic: 3 whole and 1 minced**

3 **tablespoons unsalted butter**

2 **tablespoons olive oil**

4 **tablespoons mixed minced fresh herbs, such as basil, oregano, and parsley**

12 **ounces tagliatelle**

½ **cup freshly grated Parmesan cheese**

Cut the asparagus into 2-inch lengths.

Steam the asparagus over boiling water in a covered pot until crisp-tender, about 3 minutes.

Pour the cream into a saucepan.

Add the 3 whole garlic cloves.

Cook until the garlic is soft.

Remove the pan from the heat and remove the garlic.

Melt the butter with the oil in a saucepan.

Sauté the minced garlic for 2 minutes.

Add the cream and herbs.

Boil to reduce the sauce until thickened.

Cook the tagliatelle in a large pot of salted boiling water until al dente. Drain.

Gently mix the tagliatelle, sauce, asparagus, and Parmesan together in a large bowl.

Tagliatelle with chanterelles

Serves 6
15 minutes

If you can't find chanterelles, almost any other mushroom can be used.

1 pound chanterelle mushrooms

3 tablespoons olive oil

4 cloves garlic, minced

Juice of 1 lemon

Salt and freshly ground black pepper to taste

$^1/_2$ bunch flat-leaf parsley, stemmed and minced

1 pound tagliatelle

$^2/_3$ cup (1$^1/_3$ sticks) unsalted butter, at room temperature

$^1/_2$ cup freshly grated Parmesan cheese, plus more for serving

Cut the chanterelles in half, lengthwise.

Heat the olive oil in a saucepan.

Add the chanterelles and stir well.

Stir in the garlic and sauté the mushrooms for 2 minutes.

Add the lemon juice, salt, pepper, and parsley.

Cook the tagliatelle in a large pot of salted boiling water until al dente. Drain.

Gently mix the pasta, butter, chanterelles, and Parmesan cheese together until
the butter is melted.

Serve with extra Parmesan cheese alongside.

Tagliatelle with chicken

Serves 6

20 minutes

3 boneless, skinless chicken breasts

Salt and freshly ground black pepper to taste

4 tablespoons olive oil

1 small zucchini, cut into cubes

1 cup chicken broth

Minced fresh thyme to taste

1 cup heavy cream

1 pound tagliatelle

Freshly grated Parmesan cheese for serving

Sprinkle the chicken with salt and pepper.

Heat the oil in a skillet.

Cook the chicken breasts until golden brown on each side.

Transfer the chicken to a plate.

Sauté the zucchini until tender.

Add the broth and boil until reduced by half.

Cut the chicken breasts into thin slices.

Add the chicken slices to the sauce.

Add the thyme, salt, and pepper to taste.

Add the cream and boil slowly for about 5 minutes.

Cook the tagliatelle in a large pot of salted boiling water until al dente. Drain.

Gently mix the sauce and pasta together.

Serve with Parmesan cheese alongside.

Tagliatelle with salmon in cream sauce

Serves 6

30 minutes

1 pound salmon fillets, boned, skinned, and cut into thin strips

Salt and freshly ground black pepper to taste

5 ounces snow peas, halved crosswise

1 tablespoon olive oil

2 shallots, minced

¹/₂ to 1 cup dry white wine

1 cup fish stock or chicken broth

1¹/₂ cups heavy cream

Several fresh basil leaves, cut into shreds

3 tablespoons cold unsalted butter

1 pound tagliatelle

Preheat the oven to 350°F.

Put the salmon on a baking sheet lined with aluminum foil.

Add salt and pepper.

Bake the salmon for 8 minutes.

Set aside and keep warm.

Cook the peas in salted boiling water for 2 minutes.

Drain and set the peas aside.

Heat the oil in a skillet.

Sauté the shallots until soft.

Add the white wine.

Boil to reduce by one third.

Add the stock.

Boil to reduce by half.

Add the cream and reduce heat to a simmer.

Add the basil and salt and pepper to taste.

Gently beat in the butter 1 tablespoon at a time.

Set the sauce aside and keep warm.

Cook the tagliatelle in a large pot of salted boiling water until al dente. Drain.

Mix two thirds of the sauce with the tagliatelle.

Divide the pasta among 6 plates.

Arrange the salmon strips and the peas on the tagliatelle and top with the remaining sauce.

Tagliatelle with mushrooms

Serves 6
15 minutes

3 tablespoons olive oil

1 pound mushrooms, chopped

Salt and freshly ground black pepper to taste

1 small zucchini, finely diced

1 cup chicken broth

Minced fresh thyme to taste

1 cup heavy cream

1 pound tagliatelle

Freshly grated Parmesan cheese for serving

Heat the oil in a skillet.

Add the mushrooms, salt, and pepper.

Sauté the mushrooms until soft.

Using a slotted spoon, transfer the mushrooms to a plate.

In the same pan, sauté the zucchini until soft.

Return the mushrooms to the pan.

Add the chicken broth.

Boil until reduced by half.

Reduce heat to a simmer.

Add thyme and salt and pepper to taste.

Add the cream and simmer for about 5 minutes.

Set aside and keep warm.

Cook the tagliatelle in a large pot of salted boiling water until al dente. Drain.

Gently mix the sauce and pasta.

Serve with freshly grated Parmesan cheese alongside.

Tagliatelle with walnut sauce

Serves 6
15 minutes

1 pound shelled walnuts
3 cloves garlic, minced
Salt to taste
2 tablespoons minced fresh flat-leaf parsley
$^1/_2$ loaf white bread, cubed
1 cup milk
1 cup olive oil
$^1/_2$ cup freshly grated Parmesan cheese
$^1/_4$ cup minced fresh basil
1 pound tagliatelle
5 tablespoons unsalted butter at room temperature
Freshly grated Parmesan cheese for serving
Walnut halves for garnish

Combine the 1 pound walnuts and the garlic in a mortar or food processor.
Crush or process the nuts and garlic.
Add the salt and parsley.
Mix the bread and milk in a bowl.
Put the bread in a colander set over a bowl and
press out the milk with the back of a large spoon.
Reserve the milk.
Place the moist white bread in the mortar or food processor.
Crush or process the bread.
Gradually stir in the olive oil, or gradually add it to the
processor with the machine running.
If the sauce is too thick, add some milk.
Add the Parmesan cheese and basil.
Crush or process to a smooth green sauce.
Cook the pasta in a large pot of salted boiling water until al dente. Drain.
Return the pasta to the pot.
Gently mix the butter with the pasta until the butter is melted.
Gently mix in the sauce.
Serve with Parmesan cheese alongside and garnish with walnut halves.

Tortellini

Serves 6
30 minutes + time to make pasta

Filling
12 ounces boneless, skinless chicken breasts, chopped
1 1/2 cups chicken broth
1/2 cup crème fraîche
1/3 cup freshly grated Parmesan cheese
2 egg yolks
Salt and freshly ground black pepper to taste
2 tablespoons minced fresh parsley

1 pound fresh pasta (page 22)
Freshly grated Parmesan cheese for serving
Olive oil for sprinkling

Combine the chicken and broth in a pot.
Bring to a simmer.
Remove from heat and let sit for 15 minutes. Drain.
Combine the meat and the crème fraîche in a food processor.
Process until finely chopped.
Add the Parmesan cheese, egg yolks, salt, pepper, and parsley.
Process to a paste.
Cut 2-inch-diameter rounds from the fresh pasta.
Put 1 teaspoon filling in the center of each round.
Moisten the edges and fold each circle in half.
Press the edges together to seal.
Fold one of the half moons around your left index finger and
press the points together to seal.
Place the tortellini on a tea towel that has been dusted with flour.
Repeat to make the remaining tortellini.
Cook the tortellini in a large pot of salted,
slowly boiling water until al dente. Drain.
Serve with freshly grated Parmesan and olive oil alongside.

Tortellini with spinach and cream

Serves 6
20 minutes

4 tablespoons olive oil
2 cloves garlic, minced
1 pound fresh spinach, stemmed
2 tablespoons olive oil
1 red onion, finely chopped
2 cups heavy cream
$1/2$ cup chicken broth
1 cup freshly grated Parmesan cheese
Salt and freshly ground black pepper to taste
1 pound tortellini filled with cheese or ham
Freshly grated Parmesan cheese for serving

Heat 2 tablespoons of the oil in a saucepan.
Sauté the garlic and spinach until the spinach is wilted.
Transfer the spinach mixture to a plate and let cool.
Heat the remaining 2 tablespoons oil in the same pan.
Sauté the onion until soft.
Stir in the cream and chicken broth.
Finely chop the spinach and add it to the sauce.
Stir in the Parmesan, salt, and pepper.
Cook the tortellini in a large pot of salted,
slowly boiling water until al dente. Drain.
Gently mix the tortellini and sauce in a large bowl.
Serve with freshly grated Parmesan cheese alongside.

Alfredo sauce

Serves 6
10 minutes

3 cups heavy cream
4 tablespoons unsalted butter
1 cup freshly grated Parmesan cheese
Salt and freshly ground black pepper to taste

Combine the cream and butter in a saucepan. Bring to a simmer and cook for 2 minutes. Remove from heat.
Stir in half of the Parmesan cheese. Add salt and pepper.
Gently mix the warm sauce with freshly cooked pasta and serve with grated Parmesan cheese alongside.
This sauce is also wonderful in lasagna or on ravioli.

Garlic and crème fraîche sauce

Serves 4 to 6
10 minutes

8 cloves garlic, finely chopped
1/2 teaspoon freshly ground white pepper
1 tablespoon olive oil
2 cups crème fraîche
Salt to taste
2 tablespoons parsley, chopped

Heat the oil in a saucepan over low heat. Cook the garlic and pepper for 2 or 3 minutes, or until the garlic is soft but not browned.
Stir in the crème fraîche. Simmer for about 5 minutes.
Add salt. Stir in the parsley. Serve the warm sauce with freshly cooked pasta.

Garlic and olive oil sauce

Serves 4 to 6
5 minutes

This is a typical Neapolitan sauce.

1 1/2 cups olive oil
8 cloves garlic, minced
1/2 teaspoon red pepper flakes

Heat the oil in a saucepan over medium heat. Add the garlic and pepper flakes. Cook until the garlic is lightly golden, but not brown. Mix the warm oil with freshly cooked pasta.

Pesto

Serves 6
10 minutes

2 cups fresh basil leaves (about 1 bunch, stemmed)
Pinch of salt
3 tablespoons pine nuts
$^1/_2$ cup freshly grated Parmesan cheese
2 cloves garlic
1$^1/_2$ cups olive oil

Combine the basil leaves and salt in a food processor. Purée.
Toast the pine nuts in a hot dry skillet, stirring, until they are golden brown.
Add the Parmesan, pine nuts, garlic, and olive oil to the food processor.
Process to a smooth sauce.
Add more oil if the pesto is too dry.
Mix the sauce with freshly cooked pasta.

Tomato sauce

Serves 6
10 minutes

¹/₄ cup olive oil
1 tablespoon finely chopped onion
1 tablespoon minced fresh flat-leaf parsley
2 cloves garlic, minced
2 (14-ounce) cans chopped tomatoes
Salt and freshly ground black pepper to taste

Heat the oil in a saucepan. Sauté the onion, parsley, and garlic until the onion
is soft. Stir in the tomatoes. Simmer until reduced by half.
Add salt and pepper. Gently mix the warm sauce with freshly cooked pasta.
The sauce can be stored in the refrigerator for 2 days.

Tuscan tomato sauce

Serves 6
10 minutes + 20 minutes for cooking

5 tablespoons olive oil
1 onion, finely chopped
4 cloves garlic, minced
8 to 10 fresh basil leaves, finely chopped
1¹/₂ pounds tomatoes, peeled (canned tomatoes can be used)
Salt and freshly ground black pepper to taste
1 teaspoon sugar (optional)

Heat the oil in a saucepan.
Add the onion, garlic, and basil. Sauté for 1 minute.
Add the tomatoes, salt, and pepper. Simmer over low heat for
15 to 20 minutes. Taste the sauce and add sugar if needed.
Serve the warm sauce with freshly cooked pasta, or use in other dishes.
The sauce can be stored in the refrigerator for 2 days.

Tomato pesto

Serves 6
10 minutes

¹/₄ **cup pine nuts**
¹/₂ **cup oil-packed sundried tomatoes, drained and chopped**
¹/₄ **cup freshly grated Parmesan cheese**
³/₄ **cup olive oil**

Toast the pine nuts, stirring, in a hot dry skillet until golden.
Combine the tomatoes, pine nuts, and Parmesan cheese in a food processor.
With the machine running, gradually add the oil to make a smooth sauce.
Serve as a pasta sauce or with other dishes.
Store in the refrigerator in an airtight container for up to 1 week.

Uncooked tomato sauce

Serves 6
15 minutes

Use vine-ripened tomatoes, preferably plum tomatoes.

2 pounds tomatoes
¹/₄ **cup olive oil**
2 tablespoons minced mixed fresh herbs such as basil and thyme
Salt and freshly ground black pepper to taste

Cut out the stem and cut an X across the top of the tomatoes.
Blanch the tomatoes in a large pot of boiling water for 1 minute.
Rinse the tomatoes under cold water.
Peel the tomatoes. Cut in half crosswise and squeeze and shake out the seeds.
Finely chop the tomatoes. Mix the tomatoes, oil, herbs, salt, and pepper
together. Mix the sauce with freshly cooked pasta.

Vegetable sauce

Serves 6
15 minutes

Use a mixture of fresh seasonal vegetables, preferably organic.
Try tomatoes, bell peppers, carrots, zucchini, broccoli, peas, and spinach.

1 cup olive oil
2 cups (8 ounces) chopped vegetables
Salt and freshly ground black pepper to taste
1/2 cup reserved hot pasta water

Heat the oil in a saucepan.
Sauté the vegetables for about 5 minutes.
Add salt and pepper.
Put the ingredients in a food processor.
Process to make a smooth purée.
Add the hot water.
Process to make a smooth sauce.
Gently mix the warm sauce with freshly cooked pasta.

Marinated peppers

Serves 6 to 8
45 minutes + 2 to 3 days for marinating

3 red bell peppers
3 green bell peppers
3 yellow bell peppers
2 cloves garlic, minced
1/2 bunch flat-leaf parsley, stemmed and minced
Olive oil as desired

Preheat the oven to 425°F.
Cut the peppers in half.
Remove the stem, seeds, and ribs.
Place the pepper halves, cut-side down, in a baking pan.
Bake for about 30 minutes, or until the skin bubbles and is browned.
Put the peppers in a plastic bag.
Let cool for about 15 minutes.
Peel off the skin.
Cut the peppers into strips.
Mix the pepper strips, garlic, parsley, and oil together.
Serve now as a side dish or pasta garnish, or cover and
refrigerate for 2 to 3 days to serve as part of a salad.